Words of

PATIENCE

Original edition published in English under the title
Words of Patience by Lion Publishing, Tring, England,
copyright © 1983 Lion Publishing.

First published in the United States and Canada in
1983 by Thomas Nelson Publishers.

Published in Nashville, Tennessee, by Thomas Nelson,
Inc. and distributed in Canada by Lawson Falle, Ltd.,
Cambridge, Ontario.

Photographs by Robin Bath, page 7; Sister Daniel, page
27; Fritz Fankhauser, page 31; Lion Publishing/David
Alexander, pages 29, 33, 39, 45; Paul Crooks, page 21; Jon
Willcocks, pages 9, 11 and cover, 13, 15, 17, 19, 23, 25,
35, 37, 41, 43

Scripture quotations are from the *Good News Bible*—Old
Testament: Copyright © American Bible Society 1976;
New Testament: Copyright © American Bible Society
1966, 1971, 1976.

ISBN 0-8407-5339-X

Printed in Hong Kong

Words of
PATIENCE

Thomas Nelson Publishers
Nashville • Camden • New York

GOD'S PATIENCE

The Lord is merciful and loving,
slow to become angry and full of constant love.
He does not keep on rebuking;
he is not angry forever.
He does not punish us as we deserve
or repay us for our sins and wrongs.
As high as the sky is above the earth,
so great is his love for those
who have reverence for him.
As far as the east is from the west,
so far does he remove our sins from us.
As kind as a father is to his children,
so kind is the Lord to those who honor him.
He knows what we are made of;
he remembers that we are dust.

PSALM 103:8–14

A GRACIOUS AND MERCIFUL GOD

The people of Israel prayed:
"You, Lord, you alone are Lord;
you made the heavens and the stars of the sky.
You made land and sea and everything in them;
you gave life to all . . .
But your people rebelled and disobeyed you;
they turned their backs on your Law . . .
Yet when they repented and asked you to save
them,
in heaven you heard, and time after time
you rescued them in your great mercy.
You warned them to obey your teachings,
but in pride they rejected your laws,
although keeping your Law is the way to life.
Hard-headed and stubborn, they refused to obey.
Year after year you patiently warned them.
You inspired your prophets to speak,
but your people were deaf, so you let them be
conquered by other nations.
And yet, because your mercy is great,
you did not forsake or destroy them.
You are a gracious and merciful God!

NEHEMIAH 9:6, 26, 28–31

THE LORD IS WAITING

The Sovereign Lord, the Holy One of Israel, says to the people, "Come back and quietly trust in me. Then you will be strong and secure." But you refuse to do it. . . .
And yet the Lord is waiting to be merciful to you. He is ready to take pity on you because he always does what is right. Happy are those who put their trust in the Lord.

ISAIAH 30:15, 18

SURE AS THE SUNRISE

The Lord's unfailing love and mercy still
continue,
Fresh as the morning, as sure as the sunrise.
The Lord is all I have, and so in him I put my
hope.
The Lord is good to everyone who trusts in him,
So it is best for us to wait in patience—to wait for
him to save us.

LAMENTATIONS 3:22–26

THE DAY OF THE LORD

The Lord is not slow to do what he has
promised, as some think. Instead, he is patient
with you, because he does not want anyone to be
destroyed, but wants all to turn away from their
sins.
But the Day of the Lord will come like a thief.
On that Day the heavens will disappear with a
shrill noise, the heavenly bodies will burn up
and be destroyed, and the earth with everything
in it will vanish. Since all these things will be
destroyed in this way, what kind of people
should you be? Your lives should be holy and
dedicated to God, as you wait for the Day of God
and do your best to make it come soon.

2 PETER 3:9–12

GOD'S PATIENCE—OUR OPPORTUNITY

And so, my friends, as you wait for that Day, do your best to be pure and faultless in God's sight and to be at peace with him. Look on our Lord's patience as the opportunity he is giving you to be saved.

2 PETER 3:14–15

KEEP YOUR HOPES HIGH

Be patient, then, my brothers, until the Lord comes.
See how patient a farmer is as he waits for his land to produce precious crops. He waits patiently for the autumn and spring rains. You also must be patient. Keep your hopes high, for the day of the Lord's coming is near.

JAMES 5:7–8

THE SOURCE OF PATIENCE

Everything written in the Scriptures was written to teach us, in order that we might have hope through the patience and encouragement which the Scriptures give us. And may God, the source of patience and encouragement, enable you to have the same point of view among yourselves by following the example of Christ Jesus, so that all of you together may praise with one voice the God and Father of our Lord Jesus Christ.

ROMANS 15:4–6

THE PATIENCE OF JOB

Then Job got up and tore his clothes in grief. He shaved his head and threw himself face downward on the ground. He said, "I was born with nothing, and I will die with nothing. The Lord gave, and now he has taken away. May his name be praised!"
In spite of everything that had happened, Job did not sin by blaming God.

JOB 1:20–22

A NEW SONG

I waited patiently for the Lord's help;
then he listened to me and heard my cry.
He pulled me out of a dangerous pit,
out of the deadly quicksand.
He set me safely on a rock and made me secure.
He taught me to sing a new song, a song of
praise to our God.
Many who see this will take warning
and will put their trust in the Lord.

PSALM 40:1–3

PATIENCE IN SUFFERING

Remember the prophets who spoke in the name of the Lord. Take them as examples of patient endurance under suffering. We call them happy because they endured. You have heard of Job's patience, and you know how the Lord provided for him in the end. For the Lord is full of mercy and compassion.

JAMES 5:10–11

TEST OF FAITH

Consider yourselves fortunate when all kinds of trials come your way, for you know that when your faith succeeds in facing such trials, the result is the ability to endure. Make sure that your endurance carries you all the way without failing, so that you may be perfect and complete, lacking nothing.

JAMES 1:2–4

GOD'S SERVANTS

In everything we do we show that we are God's servants by patiently enduring troubles, hardships, and difficulties. We have been beaten, jailed, and mobbed; we have been overworked and have gone without sleep or food. By our purity, knowledge, patience, and kindness we have shown ourselves to be God's servants . . . Although punished, we are not killed; although saddened, we are always glad; we seem poor, but we make many people rich; we seem to have nothing, yet we really possess everything.

2 CORINTHIANS 6:4–6, 9–10

SHARING GOD'S GLORY

We boast of the hope we have of sharing God's
glory! We also boast of our troubles, because we
know that trouble produces endurance,
endurance brings God's approval, and his
approval creates hope. This hope does not
disappoint us, for God has poured out his love
into our hearts by means of the Holy Spirit, who
is God's gift to us.

ROMANS 5:2–5

LET HOPE KEEP YOU JOYFUL

Work hard and do not be lazy. Serve the Lord
with a heart full of devotion. Let your hope keep
you joyful, be patient in your troubles, and pray
at all times.

ROMANS 12:11–12

PATIENCE REWARDED

God is not unfair. He will not forget the work you did or the love you showed for him in the help you gave and are still giving to your fellow Christians. Our great desire is that each one of you keep up his eagerness to the end, so that the things you hope for will come true. We do not want you to become lazy, but to be like those who believe and are patient, and so receive what God has promised.

HEBREWS 6:10–12

We ask God to fill you with the knowledge of his will, with all the wisdom and understanding that his Spirit gives. They you will be able to live as the Lord wants and will always do what pleases him. Your lives will produce all kinds of good deeds, and you will grow in your knowledge of God. May you be made strong with all the strength which comes from his glorious power, so that you may be able to endure everything with patience.
And with joy give thanks to the Father, who has made you fit to have your share of what God has reserved for his people in the kingdom of light.

COLOSSIANS 1:9–12

BE PATIENT WITH EVERYONE

We urge you, our brothers, to warn the idle, encourage the timid, help the weak, be patient with everyone. See that no one pays back wrong for wrong, but at all times make it your aim to do good to one another and to all people.

1 THESSALONIANS 5:14–15

NEVER GIVE UP

So let us not become tired of doing good; for if we do not give up, the time will come when we will reap the harvest. So then, as often as we have the chance, we should do good to everyone.

GALATIANS 6:9–10

LOVE IS PATIENT

Love is patient and kind; it is not jealous or conceited or proud; love is not ill-mannered or selfish or irritable; love does not keep a record of wrongs; love is not happy with evil, but is happy with the truth. Love never gives up; and its faith, hope, and patience never fail.

1 CORINTHIANS 13:4–7